NIGHTSONGS & CLAMORS

Michael Anania

MadHat Press
Asheville, North Carolina

MadHat Press
MadHat Incorporated
PO Box 8364, Asheville, NC 28814

Copyright © 2018 Michael Anania
All rights reserved

The Library of Congress has assigned
this edition a Control Number of
2018950280

ISBN 978-1-941196-75-5 (paperback)

Cover art by Marc Vincenz
Cover design by Marc Vincenz
Book design by MadHat Press

www.MadHat-Press.com

First Printing

for Anthony, who helped put this together

Other Books by Michael Anania

New Poetry Anthology

The Color of Dust

Set/Sorts

Riversongs

The Red Menace (fiction)

Constructions/Variations

Two Poems

The Sky at Ashland

Gardening the Skies

In Plain Sight: Obsessions, Morals and Domestic Laughter (essays)

Selected Poems

In Natural Light

Once Again, Flowered

Sounds/Snow

Per Enzo Agostino

Turnings

Heat Lines

Continuous Showings

Table of Contents

I.

Nightsongs and Clamors, I–VI	3
Morning Poem	9
Reaching	10
"lulled by flowers"	11
And So	12
"Shake off your heavy trance"	13
Inside Dimensions	14
Composition in Metallic Grays	16
Away So Wears	17

II.

As Seen	21
In Order To	24
Three Italian Painted Doors	27
Contingent Objects	30
Poem for Akira Blount	31
In Every Direction	32
Tristan in Felt Pen on the Rue Racine, 1996	34
An Ode	37
Durations	39
Three Poems with Max Beckmann	40
Conjecture for an October Evening	43

III.

Tin Tin Deo	47
De Un Mundo Raro	50
Dinner at the Arrayan, 11/12/11	53
Four for Orbert Davis	55
For the Fat Man	57
Autumn in New York	58
"Once on a Slender Reed"	59
Adjacent Spirits	60
Pearl Millet	62
Once More	64
In Time	68

IV.

Archways and Passages	73
Freciarossa	77
The Poet's Garden	78
from "To My Daughter, Libertà" by Michele Pane	79
Omaha Appendices V	80
Omaha Appendices VI	81
Always the Surfaces	84
Things Forgotten	87

Tampa, March 2018	90
An Afterword in Response to a Query about Gardens)	91
Notes	95
Acknowledgments	99
About the Author	101

The signs of the gods are perpetually scattered in places.
 —Simplicius

*through that frontier of doubt
crossed only by glimmers and mirages,
where language recants,
I travel toward myself*
 —Octavio Paz

I

Nightsongs & Clamors, I–VI

I hear a cry of spirits, faint and blind
… the chance of night

I.
and if I tried
    and did try,
        there is still no
code I can find
    in the sound
        of the brittle leaves
the live oaks
    are dropping
        this March night,
a rasp not quite
    like breath or song,
        a kind of absence
milled from loss,
    a game perhaps;
        we hide and seek,
press our faces
    toward sleep, the day
        still hissing in our ears

II.
a drop forge, its
    rhythms beat out
        the long night's labor,
the flash at the die's
    edge, its remnant
        dawn chipped away,
beam crane and gantry,
    between 4 and 4:05 a.m.
        the clock slows and slows;
"I wish I may, I wish
    I might" see the sun
        streak the gray skylight,
hear nothing for just
    a short while, listen
        for my self returning

III.
for Maureen Hunter

at 24th and Lake Street,
    Maureen, music heralded
        the night—Joe Turner,
Ruth Brown, The Drifters,
    Little Walter and Otis Rush—
        "all night, all night long,"
something caught there,
    the moment swaying;
        you are, all at once,
aware of your breathing,
    its measured rise and fall,
        the streetcar tracks like
a stream you can not
    cross, should not cross;
        overhead, the trolley wires
spit out arcs of light;
    they linger in your
        eyes and bite your tongue;
red neon melts into
    the damp air, sputters
        and hums along, sin
like a chorus, one promise
    after another, Dixie Peach,
        high-hat and drumhead pulsing

Michael Anania

IV.
"are we alone? and here?
    and here alone?" Rameau's
       consoling symmetries,
residual city light,
   its ingathering ash;
      night is a space, a precinct
of self we curl into;
   things rush past us, spin
      away like corn stubble,
fallow fields the highway
   reels past us, constellations
      distance holds in place;
what shall I wish for?
    "pleasant dreams," she says,
       reaching for the light

V.
"to find a pathway
    through a field of doubt,"
        one measure at a time,
determined as crystal,
    perhaps, or as unlikely
        as song; so guide me now,
Calliope, heel and toe,
    a step in prelude; words
        and weather persuade us,
move the night along;
    sparks our eyes flash
        against the darkness;
empty is its own space
    defined by what surrounds
        it, tremors and memory

Michael Anania

VI.
voices splinter against
    brickwork like shells, first
        tumbled and polished, then
shattered; sirens we know
    by heart coil and strike; elms
        flail serrated leaves here
and there; "mercy," someone
    cries, "have mercy," rain
        like a chorus, tree locusts,
the pavement's breath slow
    and uncertain, "lord, lord,
        I don't know what's gonna
make everything alright";
    one wheel on the mobile
        stretcher, chattering by

Morning Poem

an eyelash,
yours, brushes
the close threads
of a pillow-
case, mine

Michael Anania

Reaching

we thought that sudden
 was what mattered, each
  touch met with desire,

each desire equal to
 the other, chords
  progressing into chords,

music and fervor,
 breath amounting to
  song, descant and sigh

"lulled with flowers"

and can you sleep
    and sleeping dream a sudden
        aperture, irides, touch

moist quick, imagined
    petals curled downward,
        calyx, sound and sepal;

"alas," of course, "daughter
    of Aeolus," breath recalled,
        something eased along your cheek,

moonrise behind the sea wall,
    waves breaking into its
        bright and shadowed orange

Michael Anania

And So

it might have been lake water
    tapping against the boat's stern,
        the inevitable rock of still
            harbors, evening's mutual

sadness, touch as certain
    as anything; life, after all,
        is neurons firing and their
            cascading consequences, you

titled against the dark
    like wavelets rippling
        lighttips, in multiples, their
            brightness and yours, skin drawn up,

this warming chill I thought
    had been lost, breathe
        and breathe again, zephyrous,
            your hair and you coming ashore

"Shake off your heavy trance"

lavender crowns at
   the window, February
      morning rain, I am
between things once
   again, sleep and waking,
      night's stale taste and the day

Michael Anania

Inside Dimensions

> *The first seven distances are most reliable.*
> —Erwin Hubble

i.
reached inside, how far barely
matters, it was, after all, the first
intrusion and its moisture he
later said astonished him

ii.
can you keep pace with your
own anatomy, how it suffers
one change after another, your
hands no longer quite reliable

iii.
"what moves you when your
senses seem to come up empty"
time after time? the exigent world
and its radiance, its interrupted light

iv.
distances, distances—the thin line,
gray and uncertain, how weariness
has come to seem a property of those
receding figures as they plod away

v.
tonight there was a sapphire
brilliance to the western sky,
as though there were a unique
balance between day and night

vi.
we might have asked for more,
I suppose, a taste surviving taste,
something, that is, to commemorate
ourselves, fully, in the moment

vii.
as they came floating, each flower
and weed, words, words, your reach,
thinning, matters, those images mixing
dream and waking to cloud your sight

Michael Anania

Composition in Metallic Grays

Bitumen of Judea
and oil of lavender,
the slanted roofline

still barely visible;
we stare into its varied
grays and its archaic

magics, the first photograph,
shadows shadowing
the dimpled metal plate,

shaded with hours of
sunlight passing through:
wait! wait! it is, after all,

the real imposing itself
on the real; in time touch
always leaves its mark;

light is a hammer, earth
its forge, bitumen asphalt
welled up, Hephaestus

Away So Wears

i.
it is, I think, the long
slope of dreaming; you
wake from its certainties

uncertain, the emperor's
puzzle with you each morning—
which flight, which husk is this?—

its voices, so clear; still,
the light through your east
window silences them;

this is the other you, my
second self, speaking
as always, out of turn

ii.
love is what we fail at,
waking and sleeping;
it is only my own warmth,

the space under the covers,
I turn into, nothing more,
a shadow sleep leaves behind,

Michael Anania

the present absence, something
so easily made slight, morning's
brief portion of darkness;

once there was the odor of peat,
damp loam and seedlings,
the breath soil draws in

and through the long night, expels,
nymph leaf unfurling, her shape
lifting and falling beside me

II

As Seen

form and matter joined

this morning the water tumbles toward me full
of light and foam, brief lines discerned in fragments,
the sand churned, blue going toward brown and opaque;

these shapes occur and reoccur, light grown thick,
as though this tumult proposed a clarity
that we might move in and among; imagine

thought curled over itself, each thing folded inward,
time spun into threads; you wet each strand between
your fingers, unsteady, lift them one by one,

up to the needle's eye; after several
tries, passing them through future and present
perfect, the past knotted in place and held fast;

consider the still life, not *dead,* certainly,
or even inert but rather, color poised,
at once liquid and solid, orange paint raised

at the orange's edge, brush and hand implicit;
light, its light, not yours, caught in the bristles track,
an occasion of form and matter held there;

Michael Anania

space accedes to color, color to motion,
motion to gesture, each the other's moment,
each moment a force arced and snared and made still;

a table of ordinary objects oddly
skewed, as though each thing acquired a kind of force
sharing in the painting's equilibrium;

so we stand before a cascade of causes,
arranged, the table set, light from an unseen
window crossing from left to right, each shadow

darkening edges; apple, pear, the pitcher's
side raised and curved outward, insistent, cloudlike;
it is a weather, then, a landscape, arms, legs,

her head turned, bare shoulder, lines in a cloth thrown
there carelessly, fold after fold, hillside, hip,
the valley at her thigh, rainwash, her ankle;

each surface always engaging another,
flat table intersecting the flat canvas,
paint disturbing both planes, deliberation,

intended but with unanticipated
consequences, reasoning backward, effects
within effects, arbitrary, essential;

surfaces we carry with us like love songs
or grace, a condition not a quality;
part of its beauty is anticipation,

part, the way memory is confirmed and gives way
to separate occasions, crafted moments,
bright filaments the eye spins out and pulls back

Michael Anania

In Order to

> *We do not remember why this custom is performed in this manner.*
> —Nathaniel Tarn

i.
it is not a circle, not quite,
and its recurrences seem,
for the most part, accidental;
the kestrel lifts its kill, feathers
spin across asphalt, clouds
and contrails open to contrails
and clouds, blue persists; each day
I make my way beneath live oaks and cedars;
light now seems to be a compromise
the kestrel manages in waves,
substance is, in the moment at least,
unlikely, the image unmaking itself;
branch and shadow dance in the space
between their opposing harmonies

ii.
it's about time, what we carry
with us and what we discard,
stories we lose ourselves in,
their parts fluttering like rags,
cornsilk or cottonwood fluff;

perhaps, the dream we struggle
through and only partially
remember is what matters most,
waking's losses, occasions
both certain and customary;
mock orange, the camellia's
bright leaves climbing cut stone,
echinacea and salvia florencia,
after all these years, still blossoming

iii.
once in a narrow passage
between islands, after a morning's
succession of rainbows, a storm
swept over us, spindrift,
sea foam raised into a white squall;
everything was salt and light,
we held fast, turned our faces
from the wind and inhaled the sea;
it stayed in our throats for days,
the taste of it, something to share
like the brine you tip from a shell
or the way love's yeast lingers
on your tongue, part thought,
part word, part unsteady breathing

iv.
this is, I suppose, how we hold
the moment against its lapse
into time, occasions when the present
is itself a recollection, memory,
reach, desire and touch, custom;
the droplet is the mass water can hold
to itself, its husk weak and mobile,
is not so much surface as a play
of light rounded there as though
it were being carried; quick recall,
seafroth or glory-of-the-snow, blue
with white luminescent centers,
touches of Crete and Cyprus there
amid the damp loam you once knelt into

Three Italian Painted Doors

for Elaine Galen

sulla lunga controversia
un irrefutabile sigillo
— Mario Luzi

I.
Etruscus in gray stone and greening shadows.
Clouds stir. Distance seems entirely a quality
imposed by diffraction, bright imperfections

intervening between surface and surface.
Color fades to color; bare feet polish stone
door sills; alphabets we barely imagine

cut into dark tufa; voices, finger cymbals,
the light foot lifted, arms raised, *to dream,*
to imagine, to rave, an empty cup tilted.

Michael Anania

II.
Orvieto in August. Sunlight. The cathedral
gleaming. When was it piety and beauty
became the mutual qualities of light?

Memory is color, speech its brush, cloth
becomes volume, the sheen each stroke
leaves there, space contracted in time,

the dancer poised in her own brightness—
song and balance, then. Breath, its lift toward flight,
cymbal and syllable, one past and then another.

III.
A mirror turned, like a leaf, by its stem,
self, then scene—Peleus, Thetis, Helen—
your eyes, a smile, you tilt your head

into Ariadne, love's madness, again,
turning, the bronze image moving
seaward, clouded with your breath;

you would be spun into them, then,
threads of light and shadow—mirror,
cymbal, shallow cup and painted door.

Michael Anania

Contingent Objects

or slipped from one world of
possibility, of necessity, then
into another: Io is likeness
and Egypt, acceptant,
at once, of change
and certainty. Imagine,
she might have said,
and not entirely out of
nothing, things propel
themselves or are propelled
into time, if not actually
into space—in this not
wholly limited sense, if
you can recollect a moment
in the past, however recent,
in which these things came
to mind, then they occupy
a certain place in time
in the sense, of course,
that all time is past
or passing. The future
is merely an hypothesis,
the proposition that
some distant, as yet
undeveloped present,
will become past and so
take up its place in time

Poem for Akira Blount

response to a commission from John Matthias

She comes to us, arrayed
                in twigs and branches,
a figure, not of change,
                but of what change
might leave behind,
                ragged, stark, and as certain
as the darkening season,
                winter's brittle
dryad, a spirit
                in the guise of a doll.

Michael Anania

In Every Direction

for Roy Fisher

i.
a certain severity
   of light, as though
      the various parts of the scene

were stammered through
   a distant projector or textures
      shadowed across the wall

you're up against, brick-
   work and tattered posters
      AUDITO at your left

shoulder, *BAND* at your ear
   and *INGLY,* the wheat paste
      curled over like parched soil

ii.
green stretched into blue
   a brush tip engendered there,
      seen and then recalled,

or recalled and then seen,
   this scene both memory
      and proposition, almost

wordless, wind stirring
   color from the grass, you
      "think of a tree to make it last"

Michael Anania

Tristan in Felt Pen on the Rue Racine 1996

for John Montague

from St. Michele to the Place de l'Odéon—
the path student messengers took in '68—
every five or six paces in black felt pen,
Tristan inked on gray stone at eye level,
Tristan Tristan Tristan Tristan,
with an *s* not, as you might expect, a *z;*

I thought of you, John, in America
that year, went to the Rue Daguerre
to read your radiometers, see just
how much light had been expended
in your absence, in Beckett's;
"clear black," he said, darkness visible,

"squandering learning wandering burning,"
rhymes edging toward defiance and regret,
"mad Ireland," your father underground
pushing nickels on the Pelham Line, so
much to account for, so unlikely in verse,
troubles even distance can't disregard,

scuffing the Omagh Road into chaos,
the Haight into flowers and painted skin,
the Milwaukee Fourteen, the Chicago Seven,

the Buffalo Twelve, so much to be said
for poetry, Lowell, Mailer and Genet
in General Logan's equestrian path;

Tristan Tristan Tristan Tristan,
all that you escape from, the sword
he placed between them, so easily
passed over, fair Irish face half turned,
a knee raised, arm lifted homeward,
Tristopher sailing on the slow west wind;

"Cry not yet! There's many a smile"
in every uprising, many a gain in loss;
Sartre, with his hand lifted to the crowd,
explains and explains; perhaps lucidity
is the problem, inherently unspontaneous
and counter-revolutionary; treasonous

Tristan lifts her to himself; workers at Renault
stop working; in Buffalo, Milwaukee
and Chicago, in Derry, too, chants and slogans,
by fits and starts; "Frenchie," Nelson said,
and took her to a station-house lockup
and to the site of Chicago's gallows;

Michael Anania

how is it outrage and defiance warm
the heart, the taint of tear gas and cordite
lingering in her clothes, ah Bernadette,
imagined; Simone, the medallion swaying
at her throat, drab afternoon sunlight,
West Evergreen, lyrics misremembered,

the "second line" playing its slow tempo;
is it "love in death" or "love and death,"
liebestod, "just a closer walk with thee,"
poor Kleist, his Amazons among the peacocks,
feathered condoms hung up to dry, and woke
to their bright colors, a cartoon sexuality;

Tristan's chord and the transcendent principle
of closeness ("what a wonderful line, Willie,
oh something lasting woe … what now? words fail"),
each and every ending stammers toward us
as though breathlessness itself were a kind of song,
love's old sweet indigent self singing on and on

An Ode

for January 20, 2009

Water, because it is our beginning
and nothing can live without it,
is best and gold,
which flashes like fire against the dark
and measures, ounce by ounce, the world's wealth,
but if you ask me, it is the sun
that exceeds all other lights, its day,
first warm on our faces, then spread westward across the land,
lifting shadows as it goes, brightening rivers
and if there is a contest and a victory
worthy of song, it is this
contest among ourselves, tallied, finally, and today
set down, like a burden carried
for so long it had come
to seem as though it were meant to be there.
Ah, Crispus,
these million breaths
cheered into the chill January air brighten
as though change and spirit could be made,
in this moment,
visible,
sunlight and aspiration,
wind and speech radiant among us.
Fresh snow caps the red
stone steps in Springfield; in New Salem snow

Michael Anania

      drifts along rail fence lines, its swirls
         and eddies, spun against stiff
            prairie grasses; it sighs
as it makes its way among birches and maples,
hums through wintering cattails and corn stubble,
over furrows marked by plowshare and shackle,
            blood and bone.
        The wind blows as it wishes
           and you hear it,
      the breath of things quickening,
and in this new light is lifted toward song.

Durations

for Charles Tomlinson

i.
yucca, blue flax,
   piñions and their
      shadows, snakeweed;

each mesa has
   its own dialect,
      each tree its own

habit; pronghorn
   deer graze here, listen
      to feathered clouds passing

ii.
a suffix meaning
   always, another for
      just then and *just now,*

the present opening
   its own occasions
      like the stain rain-

water makes in
   dry soil, *just then,*
      just now, as ever

Michael Anania

Three Poems with Max Beckmann

1. Family Scene

How is it dread
    became a compromise?
The space between these
    figures—mother, wife, child
and you, Max, in profile,
    stylus in hand, as though
the act of scratching
    your way through each
proposed this profile,
    yourself at work but not,
it's clear, on this scene.

2. The Night

Crowded, always, day or night,
    nude dancers, their audience
wholly inattentive. Torture,
    however, has focus—the arm
    twisted or wrists tied—
and distraction, plungers
    and the horn of a gramophone.

Michael Anania

3. The Way Home

There are no spaces here,
    no vistas, bodies, faces, arms
oddly bent, everything close.
    In this dank world, you breathe
in what has been expelled by
    the inward press of others,
the policeman somehow intimate,
    not *be on with you* or *get along*
but pass through me; home is
    not your warrant but mine.

Conjectures for an October Evening

Upriver, at Blair, bridgework
    shadowed across dull water,
        semis double-clutching the grade,
the wind, leaves clamoring
    down bluff channels, water-runs
        and stiff branches—if I could hold
it all in my hand, just so,
    not something gathered
        but caught hold of in passing
like twigs from choke-
    cherry thickets or foxtails
        along a fenceline, wild chamomile,
wood sorrel, its bitter touch,
    the wet taint of torn stems, river
        marl, their tastes deepening, word
after word. Somehow these
    things are tangible, not merely
        remembered but inventions
out of memory. Out my
    window now, pine needles stir,
        and there is no connection worth
noting between this agitation
    in the dark Illinois night
        and that proposed Nebraska,
except for the season, its
    edges, things reached out
        for and persistent change.

III

Tin Tin Deo

I.
aché, not so much in
   the beat as in the space,
     the silence, not quite

silence, memory
   and anticipation,
     between one beat

and the next, the air
   above the drumskin,
     Dizzy in tropic light;

move this way, it says,
   hips and arms in flight,
     heel and toe, earthbound;

what sunlight teaches
   is darkness, darkness light,
     sepal and whispering—

Tin Tin Deo, tumbadoras,
   there in syllable and song—
     habeñera, estrella, turning

II.
Gottschalk in Havana
  in 1854 heard it, spent
    months carefully noting

the rests in the score for
  "A Night in the Tropics,"
    nearly 600 instruments,

sound like dense foliage,
  banana tree and plumeria,
    and silences etched into

their music; beat, moist
  skin and leaf's edge, light
    and shadow, the way hips

move beneath the bundle
  balanced on her head, the dirt
    track uneven, grace and purpose,

swing, implies dance,
  estrellita, the little turn
    pauses and turns again

III.
stars, above the sea's
 tumult, turn in the night
  sky, slow-dancing; palm

fronds thrash and thrash
 at the salt wind, swing over
  the wave's steady lift and fall,

kelp lines in the sand
 and brief phosphors, tropic
  air, tinged as always, with decay;

"kiss," did you say,
 the word, merely or the act?
  breath's other beat and rest,

the tongue's sway, samba,
 double and triple, the horn
  behind the brush of finger

and palm, the drumhead
 pulled taut, her abdomen,
  " tight as a melon," she said, "try it"

Michael Anania

De Un Mundo Raro

> *stand up and look at me face to face*
> —Sappho

i.
hands, Toltec or Persian,
   it hardly matters; what is
      printed there, something

to be recited or read,
   spoken out in familiar
      company, a compact

witnessed, hand to
   hand and face to face—
      stars, the moon, night

music, one breath
   and then another, face to
      face or hand to face, once again

ii.
a dove's shadow
    ripples across paving
        stones, calligraphy

flexed from its wingtip
    to the first creases of
        your palms, *nastaliq*

inked across the whorls
    of self, swept like furling
        scarves or skeins of silk

over the deeper furrows
    clutch and grasp leave there,
        tracings of fortune and desire

iii.
ceremony is, after all,
    purpose joined with place,
        harvest and weaving, gathering

sheaf and thread, colors, yarns
    spun between waxed fingers, texts
        veined as in a bright butterfly's wings;

song moves among smooth upland
    stones, *achiote*-tinted lips, the blue
        agave-spiked hillside, water falling

seaward, clamoring its own
    music under a canopy of pink
        flowers and broad green leaves

The Dancer at the Arrayan (11/12/11)

she is the heroine of her own body
—Lorca

i.
not within the song, really,
or at its edge, the single
guitar, undersized, neon-quick,

the dancer reshapes the air,
heels striking the boards she
carries with her, her syntax,

Mayan, we suppose, back
straight, shoulders squared,
cadences of mallets on stone

Michael Anania

ii.
we lean back, holding ourselves
in place, swirl a bit, settle, turn
the last swallow or two of wine

upward against the trembling
candle light, pulse, as though
a circle of tissue lived there,

momentary, the dance
in the veins, her fingers
and yours grappling with time

Four for Orbert Davis

measured, time after time, what you insisted
upon, quiet gaining its own presence; alas,
to speak at all is to presume; presumption
thus proposes speech, speech, in time, music;
Dexter Gordon, now, counts out these sentences
one after another, "Number Four" realized
you might say, one two three four, or caught in

its distinct moment, breath lifting the upward
arc of beginning, how the interior of
each phrase is opened outward, "nevertheless,"
something imagined, one note, one syllable
at a time, catch it if you can, like a wisp
of spider silk defining the shape moving
air takes, its lines streaming through your fingers;

night wind, lake water tapping out Morse signals
hour after hour, their desperate repetitions;
is there a single tap for please? *please, please, please,*
each one rebounding from the shore, hiss, then slap;
it was Dizzy with Max Roach one Sunday morning
rubbing their palms, the beat extended, hiss
and slap, first devotion, as in prayer, then jazz;

Michael Anania

jelly roll, as Leon put it, sacrament,
wine and bread curled, street sweetened, in song, wavelets
like lips, each breath, each touch at once momentary
and certain, like sound, then, known only as it
slips toward silence, notes in their own still time,
phrase or melody, the shapes anticipation
draws into the sudden clutch of memory

For the Fat Man

>February 26, 2008

I was standing on the corner
of Rampart and Canal, just
watching the people gather,
going away, going away.

You could walk through the Quarter
early in the morning and see
steam rise from gleaming sidewalks,
going away, going away,

broom straw wet and stained
coffee-brown, green shutters
pushed open, screeching,
going away, going away,

and smell the deep river
and damp cemetery lime,
and listen to hand carts clatter,
going away, going away.

I saw you, shoeless, lifted
into a brown john-boat, in your
face, the city's sorrow,
going away, going away.

Michael Anania

Autumn in New York

Is it Milt Jackson in the trees,
    bare and evenly spaced,
the wind filled with all
    that's peopled here,
the busy margin of America
    vibrating through the afternoon.

"Once on a slender reed"

rivers and their dark
    luster, creekside loam
        streaked with clay, hills
running westward, the rush
    of clouds, plow shares
        and belt-driven threshers;
pollen and chaff briefly
    golden, the sun's daily
        offerings, incendiary;
"what makes a rich
    harvest, under which
        star should you plow?'
when all your bees
    die of hunger
        and disease where
will you go to pray,
    what river, slaked
        with oil, will answer
for your mother, name
    your penance and make all
        that's broken whole again?

Michael Anania

Adjacent Spirits

i.
>adrift again
spun jetsam, *lumina,*
>>feldspar unsettled

ii.
>jasper strung in
moving shadows, turn
>>it, then, waking

iii.
>a hand raised
fingers spread against
>>layered limestone

iv.
>*Te mando flores*
on this yellow pad, moonrise,
>>song and gesture

v.
>when Cassiopeia
is at her brightest, the shore
>>lifts and lifts again

vi.
   "fears and fancies,"
agate, flint and shale, bits
    of time gone cold

vii.
   beneath the Roman
arch, bent fingers, dressing
    a table of yellow roses

viii.
   touch the sea to
your lips, the sun-drawn
    salt on warm skin

ix.
   love's crevices,
one after another, words
    and their dampness

x.
   water and ash,
you slip away, a cloud
    beneath wavelets

Michael Anania

Pearl Millet

for Leeya Mehta

i.
wind across seed crowns,
the day's heat captured there,

she walks these furrows
each afternoon, her palms

gathering in their pollen,
green going to gold,

as though her touch could
move them toward harvest

ii.
time measured by a young eye
closing, a single adult heartbeat,

the duration of a bubble
blown through bamboo,

drifting into a clay cylinder,
half-filled with still water,

the rhythm of the milling
post lifting and falling

iii.
bright yellow occasions
she lifts to her face, cheeks

streaked with them, as though
the sun moved with her—here,

now, eyelid, heartbeat, colors
curved across the bubble's frail

surface rotate and in their own
measure, parts of seconds, burst

iv.
between seed and seed, mere
soil and, what can we call it?

readiness, perhaps, grain dark
and bending on its own weight;

she, some version of you, proposed,
here only, is the field's inherent

pressure, moment against moment,
time walked out into its times

Michael Anania

Once More

> *after Bill Evans*

i.
landfall, its oddities, dark,
resolute, a change first seen
as something adrift above

the familiar line of the sea,
horizon swiftly unreckoned
by its insistences, shadowed

forward, as it were, or is,
this oncoming certainty, with
each successive wave's rise

grown more purposeful
and strange, how the familiar
unsettles the ordinary

ii.
peace, how is it held onto,
as though it were a time without
conflict, all our borders

open, green and untended,
an idea of absence, like cold,
abstractly, the absence of heat—

darkness and light, silence
and sound, yet each is
palpable; cold is cold

to your fingers and your teeth;
darkness has edge and volume,
and silence hisses in your ears

iii.
the press of blood and breath,
pulse marking time, time
itself never at rest even

when it seems to congeal
and slow, as though it might
be lifted out of its own swift

stream, a chord doubled,
moving from one hand
to the other through

silences like a bright thread
or a strand of light,
mote quick, and passed around

iv.
we make our way, make way,
in water and air, lift and fall,
salt spray warm on our faces,

music in the breeze, voices,
"but here I am again," she says,
"calyx or irides"; phosphors

cling to your skin as though
somehow intended to make you
luminous, conspicuous, in some

small part, at least, divine;
quick trails in crystal, cloud
chambers, the heart struggling

v.
I wanted to say something
about drift and consequence,
to touch briefly on causality,

how the thread of things
twists like foam at a wave's
curl and falls, each complex

occasion, at once lost
and recurrent; sometimes
in morning light, strands

of bright spiderwebbing edge
the mainsail, the wind's force
in bright lines there, and visible

Michael Anania

In Time

for Ed Colker

throw some part of your life after birds
—Zukofsky

somehow, beginning at
the quill-tip, the feather
turns open, then closes;

what we read there,
as the wings lift
and fall, light caught

hold of, occasions
of self, futures;
is there a past that

is inherently avian,
something that moment
by moment, point

after point, offers
us a line we can
follow to its end,

to our endings; I
return to the curves
they draw in air,

filaments recalled
merely, relied on,
their purposes, ours,

lift and glide, one
arc after another;
the river furls its

slowly gathered soils
from bank to bank;
clouds, sun-swept,

brighten the day
with shadows, flight
compels both hand

and breath, word
and picture; if you
could draw on water,

Michael Anania

write on air, if speech
and flight remained
suspended there:

desire, love, sorrow,
the sudden rush of
wings in aging hands;

these spaces are intimate,
then, time's reckonings
shared, colored radians,

breathless, you might say;
already with us, light-quick,
bunting, hawk or swift,

the reach of live oaks,
their leaves trembling
between sun and shade

IV

Archways and Passages

for Phillip Trussel

I.
*"when all things mix
and the dreamers dance,"*
shadows sorted
into mottled light,

arms, breasts and thighs,
his reach and her forward
glance, blackened particles
silvered and falling, light

or shade in consequence
of sight, as Parrish might
have imagined them at play
their arching clarities,

or Poussin out of Bion
and Appellius, the long
slope of Arcady, fields
greening toward shade;

drifted, then, as though gods
and heroes might once again
preside, slim adolescent, nymph,
or satyr; now, the sudden curl

of seawater, darkening bright
sand, its breath opening damp
pores, a pale arm strung with
kelp, flexed against Okeanos;

dreams fluttering like pages
in the wind, words and leaves
spun, their masque played out,
garden scents; which cap, whose

bells? song, its airy architectures
as certain as stone, each lively
in its own sweet time, or the torque
centered in the bud, flowering

II.
that said, winter evening light
caught here among darkening
cedars and held fast, the frayed
black strands of shagged bark

counted out as rests, something
we measure for ourselves, hands
extended, as though in reaching
we could play the air itself, rhythms

those other figures might sway to,
spaces marked in time, the wind
as the right arm lifts, branches,
proposing a kind of yearning;

line is always narrative, one
cause and then another, effects
dreamed or wished into place;
the Doge, lampblack in shadow,

all that seems likely remains,
a question of intent, marks
the bristles chisel toward fable,
how we linger, like dust, in the light;

to leave the known world and pass
into what world, a latticework
of systems snarled within systems,
particulars hived around us, change,

touch hoped for, as though its arc
could be followed through space,
its chill always sudden, surprising,
the way the liquids of painting

Michael Anania

and photograph pause for us,
their occasions not so much certain
as probable, outcomes of hand, eye,
light, arm, tablature and breath

Frecciarossa

tissues wadded on the window ledge, a field
of olive trees, Tuscan light, bare winter vines,
their stakes oddly angled over broken soil,

Etruscan shadows, *copertura,* dovecotes
carved into pale tufa, *columbaria,*
what remains is ash and flight, a sheep's liver

memorialized in bronze, a thousand bobbins
balanced, cut and spun, stray fibers on their lips
and in their braided hair, spit-moistened fingers;

one mountain in haze, *parrocchia mia,*
and then another, the sea tasting of skin,
its incoming early-morning salt and yeast

Michael Anania

"The Poet's Garden"

>Van Gogh, 1888

a tumult of wildflowers
and native grasses, Petrarch
imagined them in mid-summer

not in Arles but in Avignon,
Virgil's transplanted apple
trees and white hawthorn;

petals weighted with color
reach toward us, as though
we might be their sunlight;

sight bestows its own hues,
these centuries and more
delved into, interrupted, known

NIGHTSONGS & CLAMORS

from "To My Daughter, Libertà" by Michele Pane

... At Adami you will find your Uncle Luigi
with Aunt Carlotta, Aunt Maria and Marianna.
They will tell you of your sainted Grandmother
(and Aunt Felicia will come up from Accaria),
and show you the places I left behind, all so
dear to me; though I may never be there again,
I can tell you how to recognize them, know
them as brother and sister, and understand.

Kiss the walls of the old house for me,
the little log-end I sat on by the fire.
Kiss your aunts and dear Uncle Luigi
evening and morning, a hundred times an hour.
See if you can find in the papers in the library
some scribble left there from my youth,
then you will sense the fragrance and harmony
of my life, which now seems without value.

When you hear the morning bell's cry,
jump out of bed, throw open the balcony
casement, greet the sun rising in its majesty
from Cariglione up into the deep blue sky.
Oh what leaps his daily greetings took
when he was green (but ... how many years ago?),
your father, grown old now, yet in this at least unchanged,
still a "Calabrese," dear Libertà....

Chicago, Ill. 8 April 1937

Michael Anania

Omaha Appendices V

My father's brother Frank was the second
Frank born to my grandfather and grandmother,
just as my great grandfather was the second
Angelo Michele; each had a brother who died.
That's how it was said when people talked
about their families—*there are six of us,
five who lived and one who died*—the earlier
Angelo or Frank somehow always present
in the life of his double. Names are ways
of keeping your place in the patrimony,
a space each of them shared with a gravestone,
so when my Uncle Frank named his first son
Frank, he named him, not for himself alone
but for his dead brother, and when my brother
was born, he was named Frank for two uncles,
one living and one dead in infancy
though my mother was allowed to believe
that he was also named for her step-father,
a Frieslander, by then also dead.
My Uncle Frank was dapper with a thin
Harry James moustache and pompadour.
He shaved twice a day, my mother said,
once in the morning and once at night.
In pictures he always seemed slightly turned,
as though he were just noticing as it
clicked that there was a camera aimed his way.

Omaha Appendices VI

In July 1946 or 1947 my grandfather
had a picnic at his farm in North Omaha,
just one hill west of the Mormon Monument—
two lean Mormons staring down, an infant
swaddled in a bronze grave at their feet.
He dug a trench in the farmyard, filled it
with meat and poultry wrapped in wet burlap,
corn and new potatoes, snap peas and beans,
then set logs and branches on fire on top
of the pit; it burned, then smoldered for days.
Rose, my step-grandmother, stood, as she did
every day, stirring at pots in the kitchen,
tomato sauces, ragùs, stewed chicken,
chopped meats tied in gut under boiling scum.
Everyone was there, aunts, uncles, first, second and third
cousins, Rose's family, who were also cousins,
my grandfather's friends, cousins, as well,
once, twice, three times removed, old men
with hard, thick hands, who wore khakis and white
dress shirts open at the neck, brown dress shoes,
pale brown socks, dove-gray and brown fedoras.
They sat in a circle in the farmyard—
as I sometimes sit now—their forearms
resting on their thighs, their hands curled
between their legs, speaking Calabrese
and English, sentences beginning in one

language and ending in the other.
At six or seven I understood everything
they said and almost nothing they meant.
Their wives, in mourning for life—black crepe
dresses, thick stockings and black, laced shoes—
moved up and down the farmhouse steps, full
of purpose, their hands and arms always filled.
My mother and aunts stayed mostly in the house.
My father, in his last years, black slacks, white
shirt, a dark vest unbuttoned and his gray hat,
went from the circle of old men to the circle
of brothers and brothers-in-law, his cousins,
young men just back from the War, lean and edgy,
my Uncle Frank, *Life* magazine's "Omaha
guy on Omaha Beach," stiff with shrapnel,
my Uncle Tony, home from the Philippines,
stabbed, he said, forty times in the heart,
just out of the frame on Iwo Jima.
Children of all ages buzzed through everything.
I sat on the sprung iron seat of a disk harrow
to watch my uncles rake the coals off the pit
and lift the steaming food out with pitchforks.
There were tables of planks on sawhorses,
oil cloths where the food was dumped out in mounds,
great pots of sauces, *bollito misto*
in their own pools of gray water, chicken

roasted and stewed, beer and pop in wash tubs.
Manga, my grandfather said, an invocation.
Gratia plena, we all replied; someone
said a prayer for the dead, and we ate
all afternoon in the Nebraska swelter
in a corner of Omaha still called Florence Station—
Ananias, Bonaccis, Scalzos, Gigliottis, Marascos,
Molinos, Peris, Saccos, Mangamellis, Tomainos,
Pellegis, Costanzos, Budas, Baratas, Barrettas.

Michael Anania

"Always the Surfaces"

for Diane Wakoski

1.
glass photo plates
   propped against the wall:
      skeins of shadows
and their shadows

2.
"someone called, saying,
   I found some stuff in back
      of an old storefront,
pictures of some kind"

3.
MacKenzie's soldiers,
   family portraits, board-
      walks and buckaroos,
mounds of buffalo skins

4.
all equally real in
   their own moments,
      bits of tarnished silver,
light stirred and settled

5.
into a scrim of wet
   cotton, as though
      a surface in time had been
seined in and held there

6.
"in angled stillness,"
   lives paused and bent
      inward, their eyes
fixed in darkness

7.
shades looking toward us,
   certain that something
      waited beyond the brass
cap and the iridescent lens

8.
how thin they are,
   these hard reckonings,
      lined cheeks, tight lips,
homespun and cottonwood

Michael Anania

9.
opacity is brightness,
    after all, the darkest hues
        are faces, pale hands folded
into the wide world's varied grays

10.
layers of ash, not much
    more, dust you might draw
        your finger through,
the present touch exceeding all others

Things forgotten

> ... *stay forever young and beautiful*
> —Robert Walser

once in another city,
   streetlights haloed with
      rainwater, the asphalt,

onxy for a moment
   or two, you, any you,
      forgotten, perfected;

still, it's the proposition
   that matters more than
      memory, insistent images

curled round the droplets
   in your hair or raised like
      opals along your cheeks;

damp grass, a Norway
   spruce, its needles rain-
      tipped and luminous, as well;

June; not far off, a stream
   swells and murmurs,
      a lock of wet hair falls

Michael Anania

   across your face, you lift
      it back carefully, as though
         part of a string instrument,

   reordering, for the moment
      at least, the rain, its clamors
         harmonic, recomposed;

   it is not the ecstatic
      I'm reaching for here,
         a hand or a sentence merely

   invading a bright
      occasion, but the recognition
         that something has emerged

   from what I thought of
      as set of random images,
         the passing delights myriad

   droplets make possible,
      so what if what has been
         proposed is seen, constructed

out of memory certainly
    but not remembered, not
        called up or recollected,

an invention for the past,
    the *you* grown specific,
        an *I,* of course, implied,

each present in this
    invented time filled
        with refracted light

Michael Anania

Tampa, March 2018

I notice during
    a poetry reading
        a smear of blood

on the edge
    of my file folder,
        then, an even more

distinct droplet on
    the margin of a poem
        that begins with a line

from Lucretius,
    "to find a pathway
        through a field of doubt."

I bleed easily
    these days, my skin as
        frail as onion skin.

Time in the body,
    in aging skin, is
        another form of time.

An Afterword in Response to a Query about Gardens

Gardens are like poems. The most beautiful poem? The best? Your favorite? If you read poetry seriously and broadly, the only answer is "it depends." It depends on when you read or reread the poem, why, if it's familiar, you return to it, whether you want tranquility, reassurance, passion, subtlety, balance, pathos, ecstasy or chaos. So gardens have different valences just as poems do, differing values, some of them very similar to the differing values of poetry—symmetry, harmony, disorder, wildness or any and all of these mixed together. "A green thought in a green shade" or a riot of pollen-rich flowers, large showy blooms, dahlias, peonies, neon bright zinnias, lush tropical plants or broad stretches of lupines, succulents, sea poppies, ground cover or subtle alpines, rock gardens, water gardens—the choices are as varied as gardeners, who intervene in nature in degrees as wide ranging as our interventions in language.

My own favorites: my wife's several gardens at our house in Illinois, of course—the long "L" shaped stretch of peonies along the front fence, preceded in the same beds in early spring by perennials, glory-of-the-snow, wind flowers and grape hyacinths; the garden of Dutch irises and tulips that circled the conservatory; the two oval gardens of hybrid tea roses or the naturalized daffodils, crocuses and paper whites under the hedge; the shade garden of ferns and lilies of the valley, the foxglove and delphinium garden at the bottom of the yard and the bordering lilacs. For very different, but equally personal reasons, my mother's kitchen garden in Omaha, barely eight feet by two feet, mixed flowers and vegetables tended with devotion.

Others, certainly, some of them quite notable, but in every case the beauty, if that's the right word, is enmeshed in the occasions when I was involved with them. Examples? Why not, but without hierarchy: the garden at the Casa de la Torre in Puerto Vallarta, a perfect calm in the middle of the city's clamor, with bright, cascading plants in permanent bloom and fountains all around; the garden of the Villa Sciacciapenseri outside Siena, symmetrical and well-mannered; the Elizabethan gardens on Roanoke Island in Virginia; the cactus gardens at the Museum of the Desert in Arizona; the mixture of demi-gods, plants and monsters in the tumbling water garden at the Villa Lante in Viterbo; the boxwood framed rose garden at Allerton House in central Illinois; the butterfly garden at the Museum of Science in Boston; the gardens of the Pitti Palace, politely insisting on a world of stability and order; the Butchard gardens on Vancouver Island in Victoria, BC, lush and politely abundant; the Lady Bird Johnson Wildflower Center, spare as gardens go, strictly native and sustainable with the hard Texas soil always evident; the Japanese garden in Boca Raton arguing for close gestures and subtlety; the formal gardens backed by a great open swale at the Vaux-le-Vicomte outside Paris, the roof garden of the Kraft Hotel in Florence where I was quite ill and in its precincts recovered.

Marvell's "annihilating" notwithstanding, every garden is a made place with boundaries. The foregrounds of quiet knowledge they offer us are at once certain and provisional. Unlike poems, though and maybe sadly so, gardens have to be tended and remade. Leave a garden for a year or so and it will go feral, slipping back into the prairie or the marshland that preceded it. Their moments of significance, of beauty, are just that, moments. Insistently temporal, gardens are surfaces in time.

Notes

"Nightsongs and Clamors"—"I hear the cry…," Sydney
  "the chance of night," Campion
  Rameau, from his *Castor and Pollux*.
  "to find a pathway…," from Lucretius

"As Seen"—"form and matter joined," Dante, *Paradiso*.

"In Order to"—"We do not remember…," from Nathaniel Tarn's *The Beautiful Contradictions*.

"Three Italian Painted Doors"—Mario Luzi, "over the long controversy/ an irrefutable seal."
  "a mirror…," Etruscan hand mirrors had mythic scenes in relief on their backs.

"In Every Direction"—"think of a tree to make it last," from Lorine Niedecker's *New Goose*.

"Tristan in Felt Pen"—"Pelham Line," Montague's father worked in the New York subways.
  "Frenchie," Nelson Algren's nickname for Simone de Beauvoir.

"Tin Tin Deo"—a 1947 Afro-Cuban Dizzy Gillespie cut with Chano Pozo.

aché—in Santeria, the essential energy of the world, which is manifested in the body.

Gottschalk, Louis Moreau Gottschalk, American pianist and composer (1829–1869), traveled to Cuba and Latin America in 1854.

"De Un Mundo Raro"— a Spanish song by Chebela Vargas.

"Four for Orbert Davis"— "as Leon put it...," the identity of the sacrament and jelly roll is from Leon Forrest's novel *The Bloodworth Orphans*.

"For the Fat Man"—For a time, during Hurricane Katrina, it was rumored that Fats Domino had died in the storm; later, he was filmed alive, being lifted into a fishing boat.

"once on a slender reed"—Virgil, from the abandoned opening of the *Aeneid*.

"when all your bees...," from the account of Aristaeus in *Georgics* IV.

"Archways and Passages"—"*when all things mix/and the dreamers dance,*" Robert Duncan.

"Frecciarossa"—"sheep's liver...," an Etruscan model liver used to teach the auguries.

"To My Daughter, Libertà"—text from Michele Pane, *Musa Sylvestra* (Bonacci Editore, Roma).

Acknowledgments

Grateful acknowledgment to the following publications in which some of these poems first appeared: *Valley Voices, Notre Dame Review, Jet Fuel Review, Guest Room, Toad Suck Review, Briar Cliff Review, december, Fifth Wednesday, New American Writing,* and *Plume.*

"To My Daughter, Libertà" was first published in *Gathering/Fifteen Poets/Poems,* a portfolio with lithographs by Ed Colker, by Haybarn Press (2010).

"As Seen" was first published in *angles & naked vision,* a portfolio of poems with lithographs by Ed Colker, by Haybarn Press (2016).

About the Author

MICHAEL ANANIA is a poet, essayist, and fiction writer. His published work includes thirteen collections of poetry, among them *Selected Poems* (1994), *In Natural Light* (1999), *Heat Lines* (2006), and *Continuous Showings* (MadHat Press, 2017). His work is widely anthologized and has been translated into Italian, German, French, Spanish and Czech. He has also published a novel, *The Red Menace*, and a collection of essays, *In Plain Sight*. He has received a number of awards and fellowships, including the Charles Angoff Award and the Aniello Lauri Award for poems in this collection.

Anania was poetry editor of *Audit, a quarterly*, founder and co-editor of *Audit/Poetry*, poetry and literary editor of The Swallow Press, poetry editor of *Partisan Review* and a contributing editor to *Tri-Quarterly* and has served as an advisory editor to a number of other magazines and presses.

He is Professor Emeritus of English at the University of Illinois at Chicago and a member of the faculty in writing at Northwestern University. He also taught at SUNY at Buffalo and the University of Chicago. He lives in Austin, Texas, and on Lake Michigan.

www.ingramcontent.com/pod-product-compliance
Lightning Source LLC
Chambersburg PA
CBHW020335170426
43200CB00006B/396